EASY PIANO

Jonas  *Brothers*

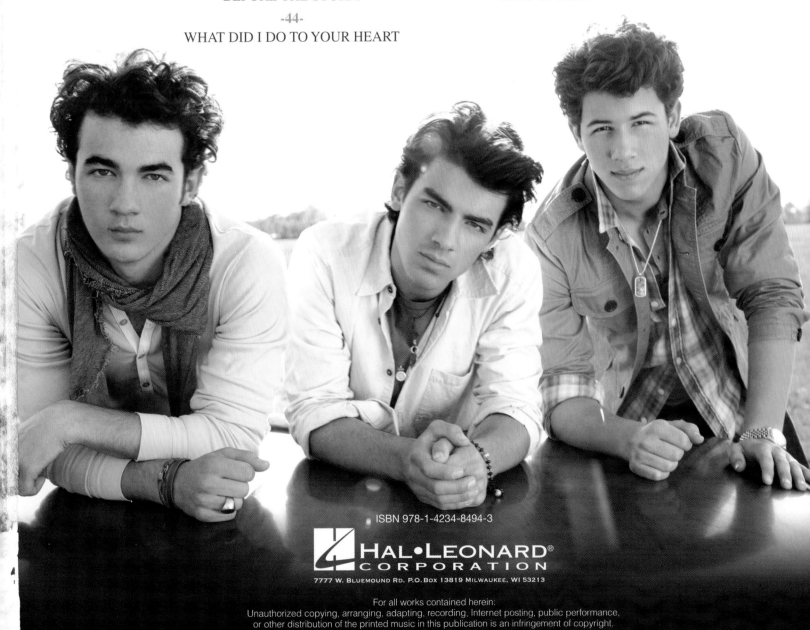

ISBN 978-1-4234-8494-3

HAL•LEONARD®
CORPORATION
7777 W. BLUEMOUND RD. P.O. BOX 13819 MILWAUKEE, WI 53213

Visit Hal Leonard Online at
www.halleonard.com

WORLD WAR III

Words and Music by
NICHOLAS JONAS

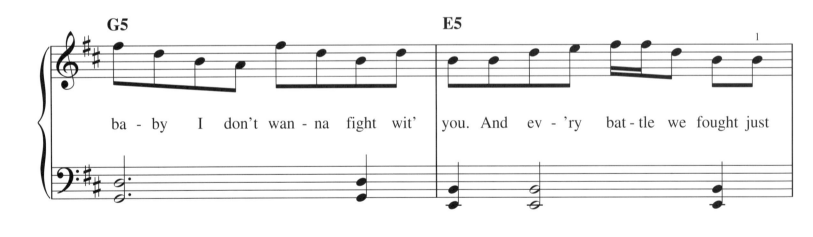

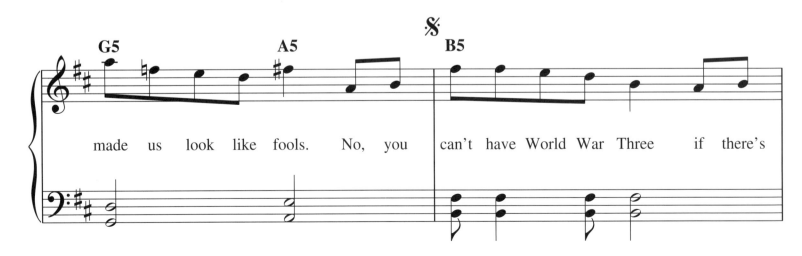

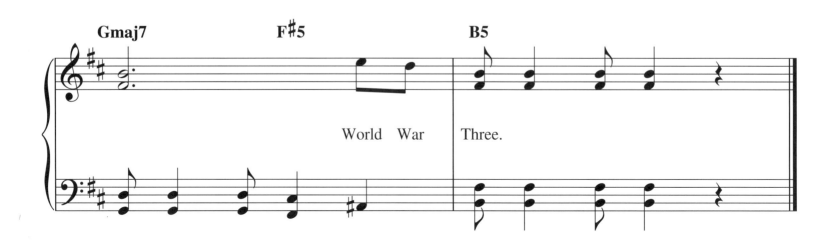

PARANOID

Words and Music by NICHOLAS JONAS,
JOSEPH JONAS, KEVIN JONAS II,
CATHY DENNIS and JOHN FIELDS

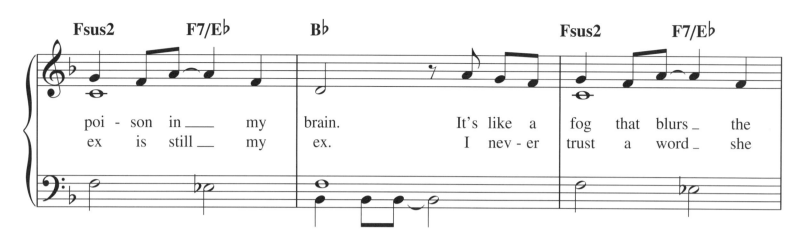

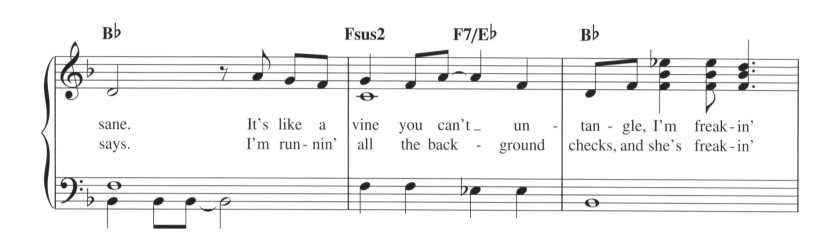

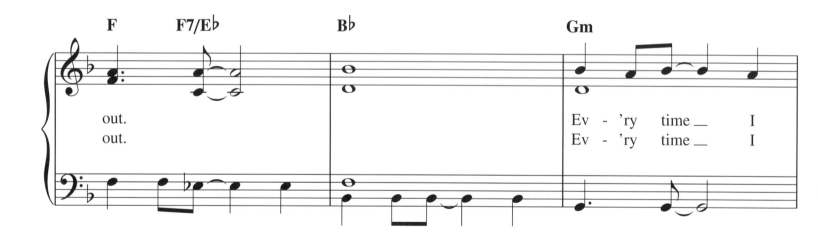

FLY WITH ME

Words and Music by NICHOLAS JONAS,
JOSEPH JONAS, KEVIN JONAS II
and GREG GARBOWSKY

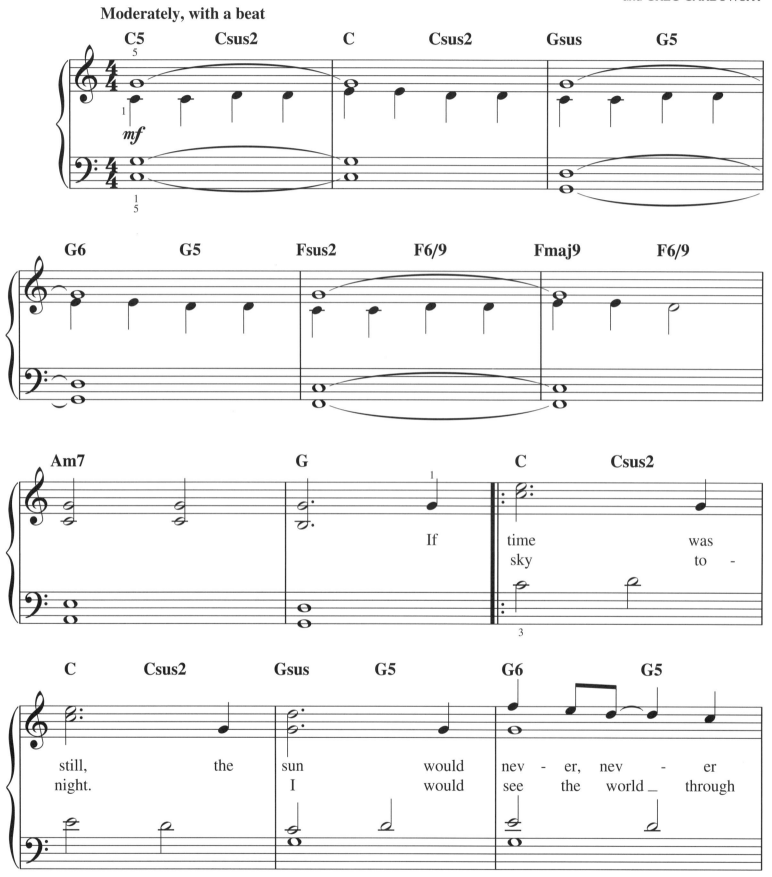

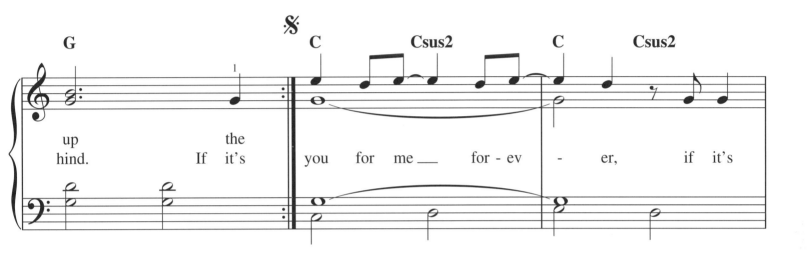

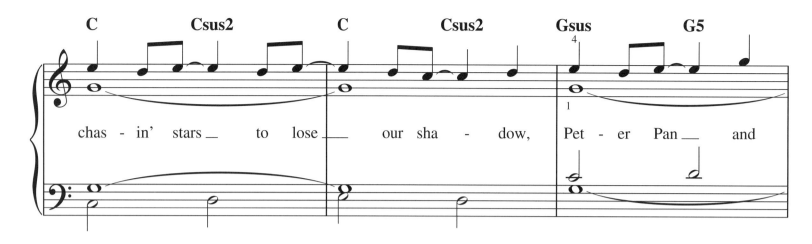

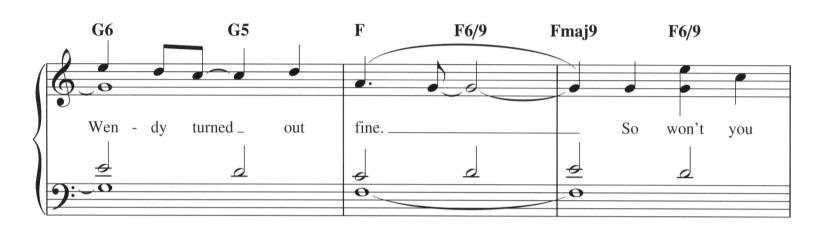

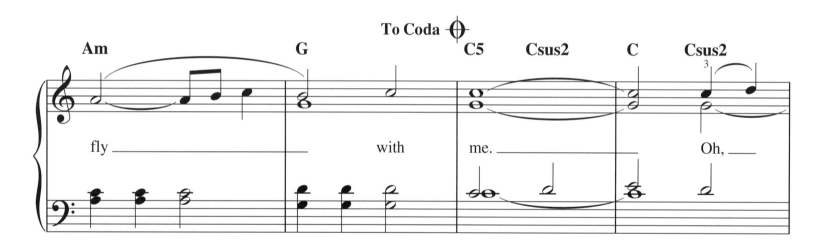

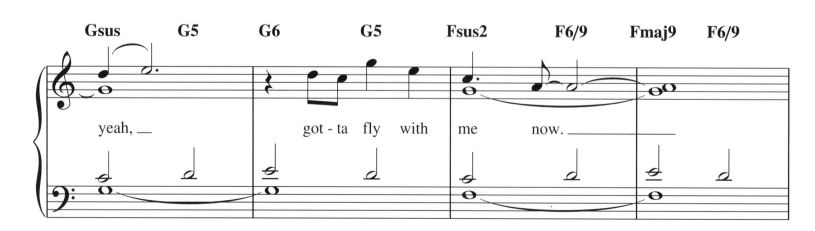

D.S. al Coda

once a - gain. _____ If it's

CODA

Am7 me. May - be you were just __ a - fraid know - ing

G

F you were miles __ a - way from the place where __ you

Am7 need - ed to be. ____

G And that's

Am7 right here with me. __

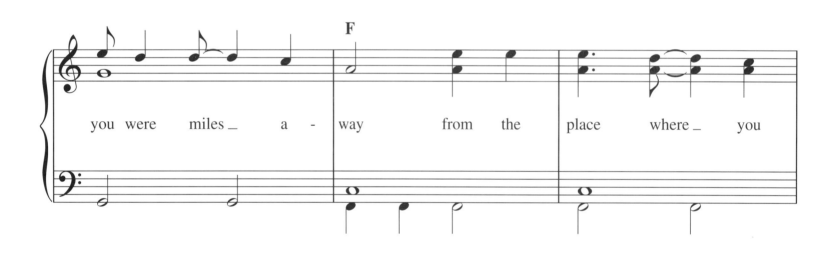

POISON IVY

Words and Music by NICHOLAS JONAS,
JOSEPH JONAS, KEVIN JONAS II
and GREG GARBOWSKY

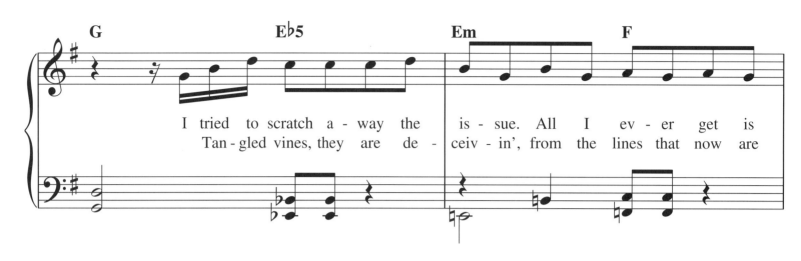

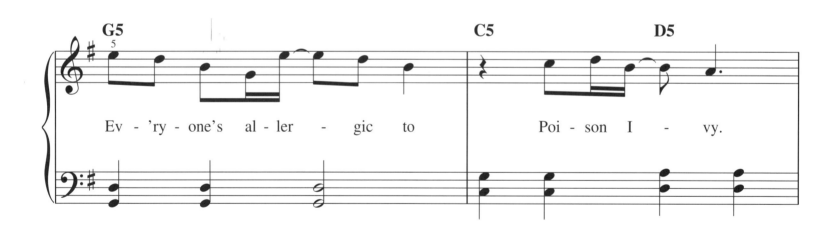

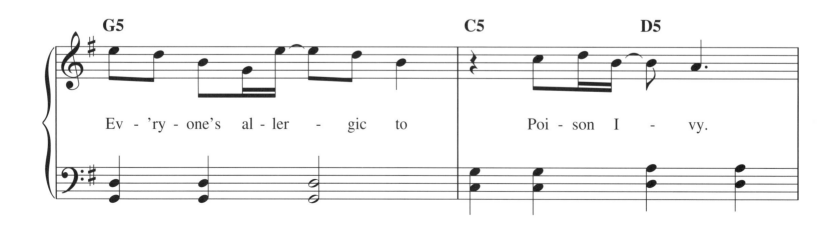

I can't stop e-ven if I try, lay down my pride. I can't walk a - way.___

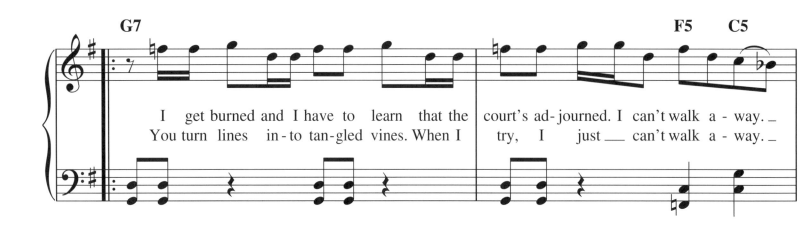

I get burned and I have to learn that the court's ad-journed. I can't walk a - way.___
You turn lines in-to tan-gled vines. When I try, I just ___ can't walk a - way.___

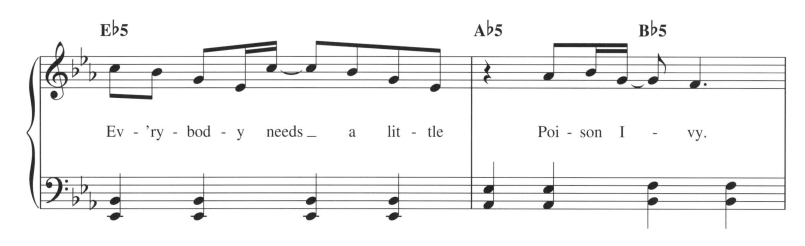

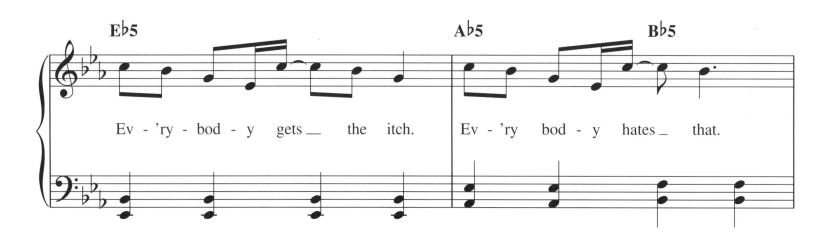

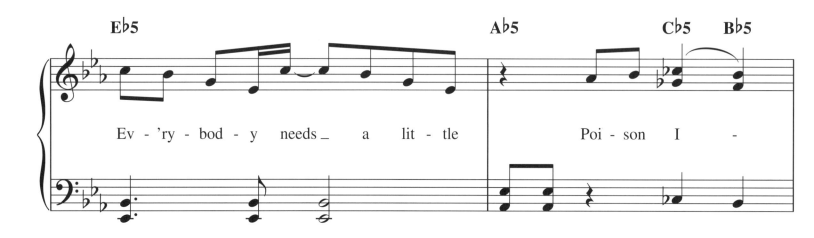

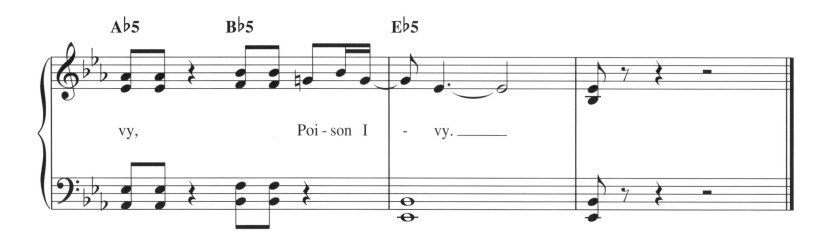

HEY BABY

Words and Music by NICHOLAS JONAS,
JOSEPH JONAS and KEVIN JONAS II

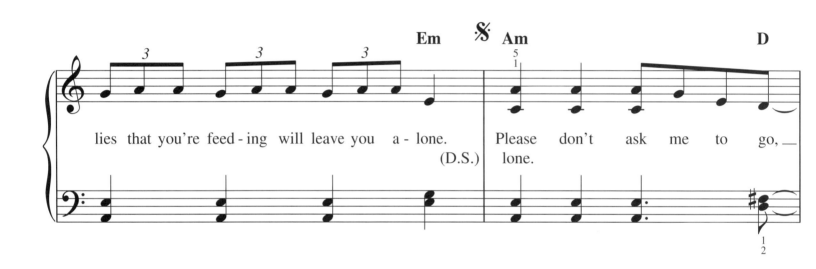

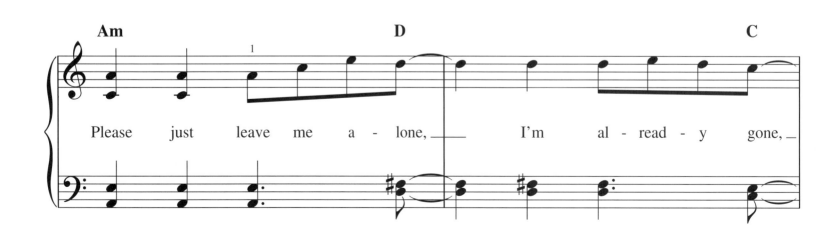

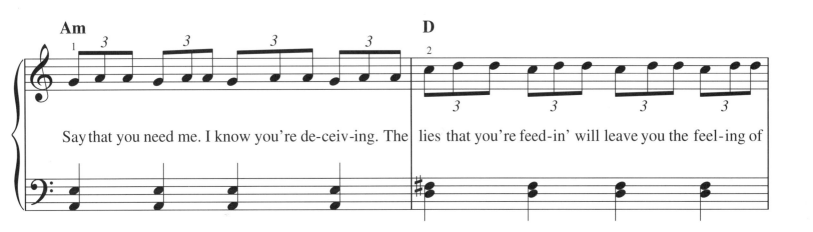

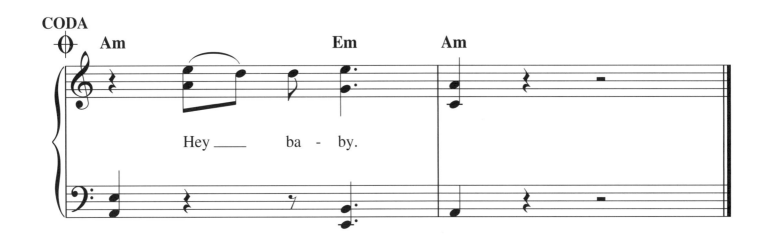

BEFORE THE STORM

Words and Music by NICHOLAS JONAS,
JOSEPH JONAS, KEVIN JONAS II
and MILEY CYRUS

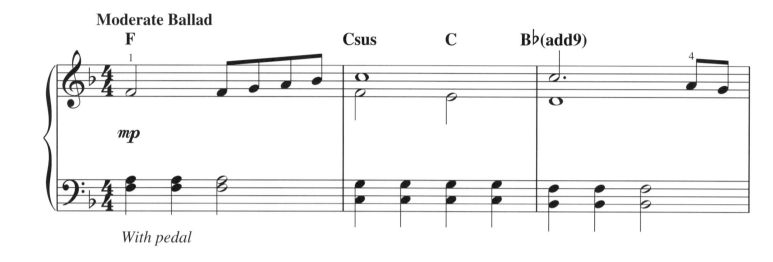

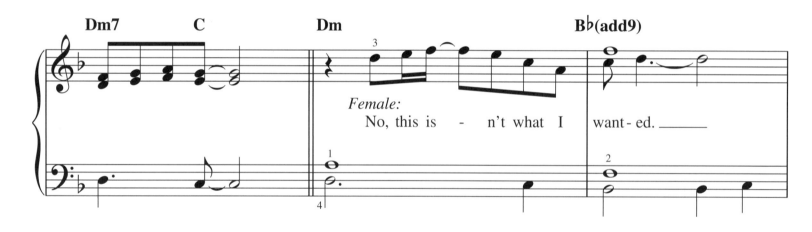

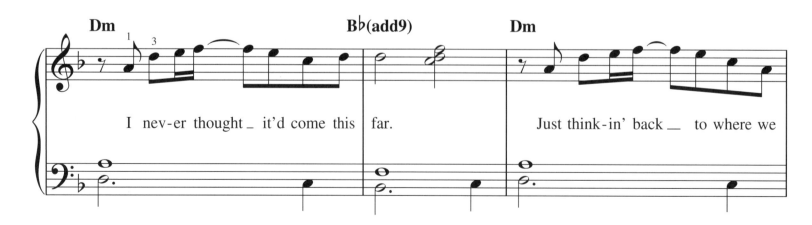

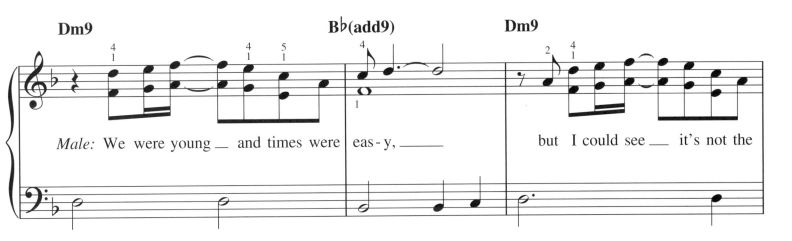

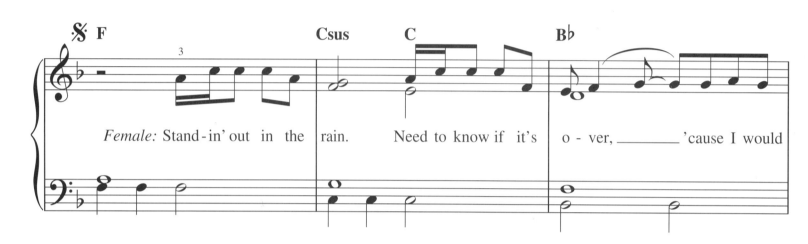

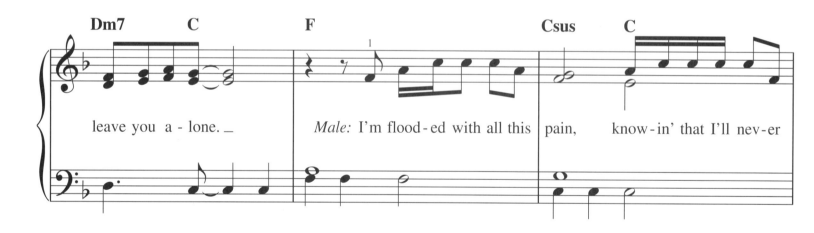

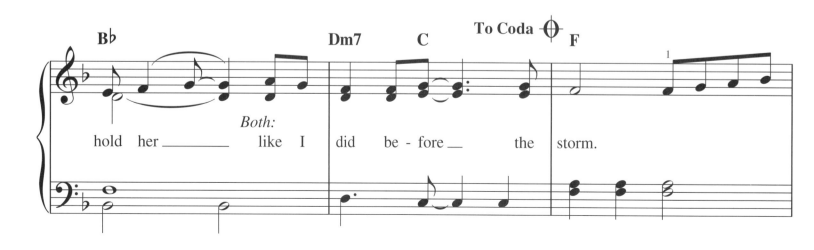

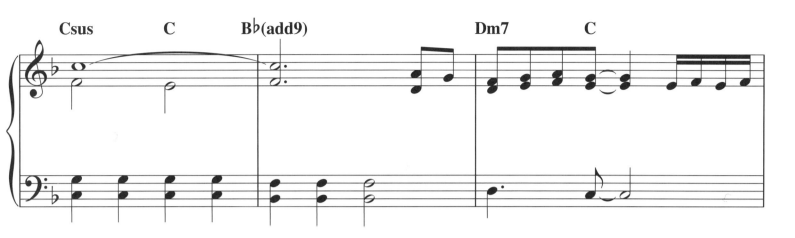

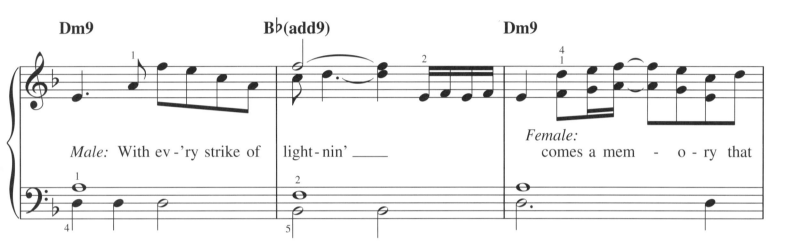

Male: With ev-'ry strike of light-nin' ___ *Female:* comes a mem - o - ry that

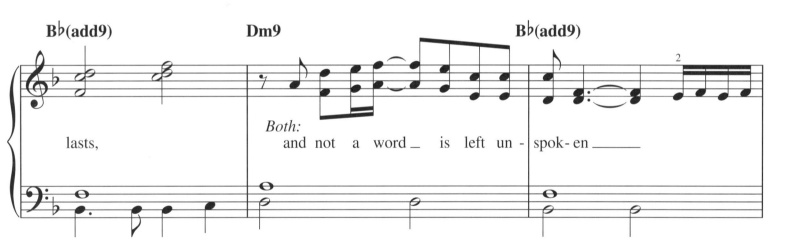

lasts, *Both:* and not a word_ is left un - spok-en ___

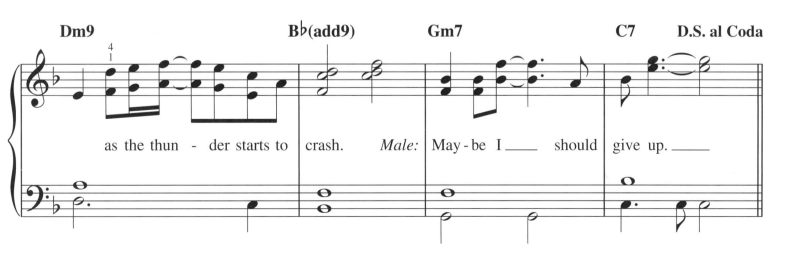

as the thun - der starts to crash. *Male:* May-be I ___ should give up. ___

CODA

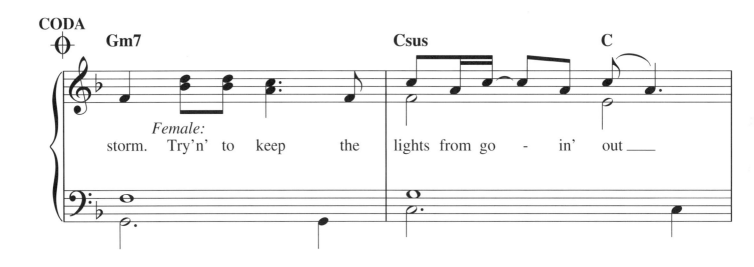

Gm7   **Csus**   **C**

Female:
storm. Try'n' to keep the lights from go - in' out ____

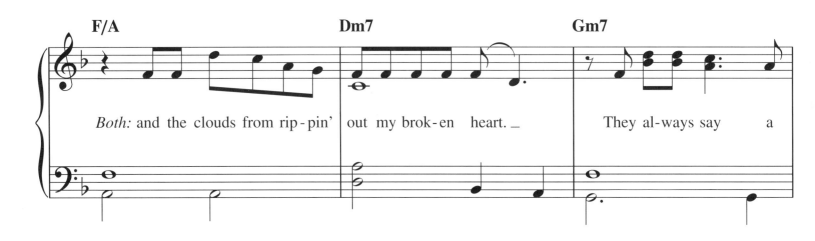

F/A   **Dm7**   **Gm7**

Both: and the clouds from rip-pin' out my brok-en heart. _ They al-ways say a

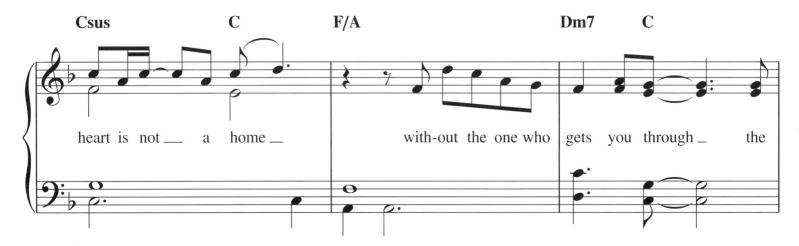

Csus   **C**   **F/A**   **Dm7**   **C**

heart is not __ a home __ with-out the one who gets you through _ the

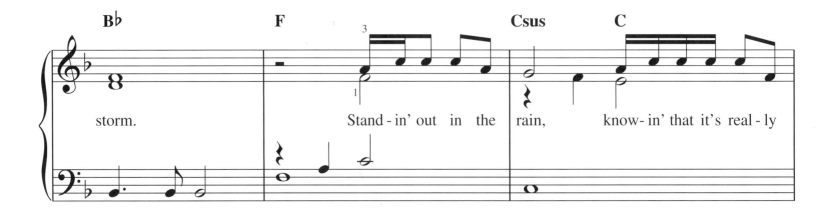

B♭   **F**   **Csus**   **C**

storm. Stand - in' out in the rain, know - in' that it's real - ly

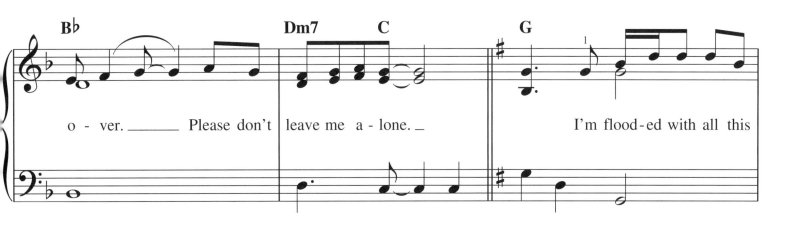

o - ver. _____ Please don't | leave me a - lone. _   I'm flood-ed with all this

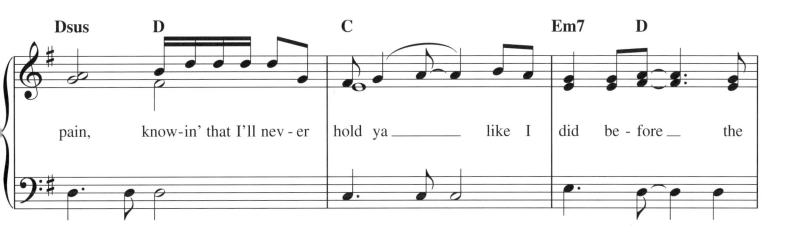

pain,   know-in' that I'll nev - er | hold ya _____ like I | did be - fore _ the

storm, _____ | _____ *Female:* yeah, _____

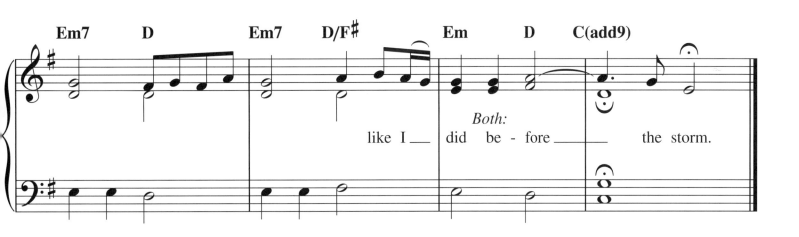

Both:
like I __ did be - fore _____ the storm.

WHAT DID I DO TO YOUR HEART

Words and Music by NICHOLAS JONAS,
JOSEPH JONAS and KEVIN JONAS II

Energetic Pop Rock

Ba - by girl, I'm just a
All I ev - er get is

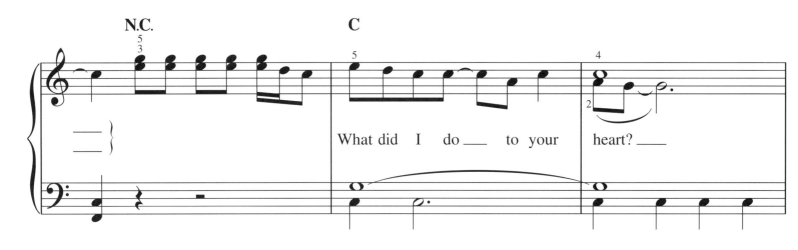

What did I do ___ to your heart? ___

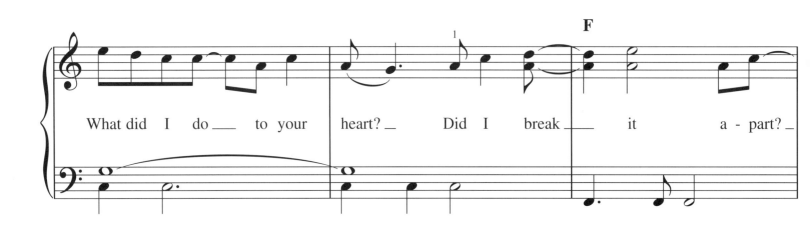

What did I do ___ to your heart? ___ Did I break ___ it a - part? ___

___ Did I break ___ it, your heart? ___ ___

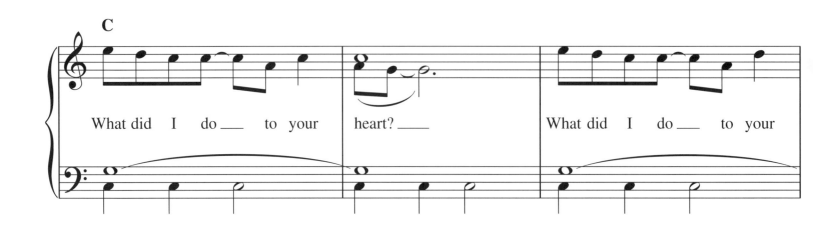

What did I do ___ to your heart? ___ What did I do ___ to your

MUCH BETTER

Words and Music by NICHOLAS JONAS,
JOSEPH JONAS and KEVIN JONAS II

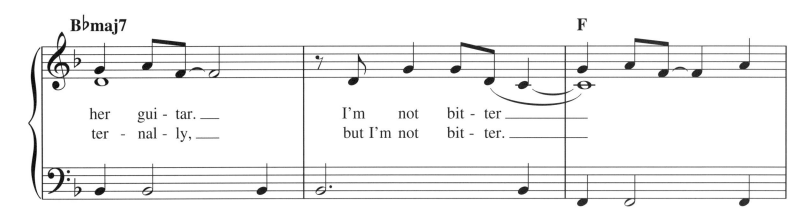

BLACK KEYS

Words and Music by NICHOLAS JONAS,
JOSEPH JONAS and KEVIN JONAS II

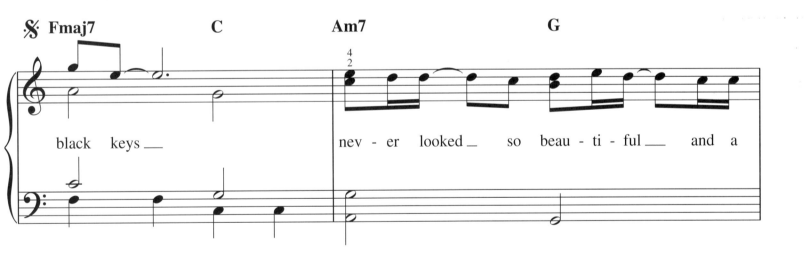

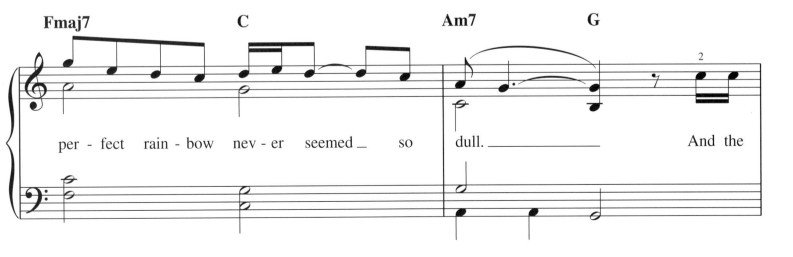

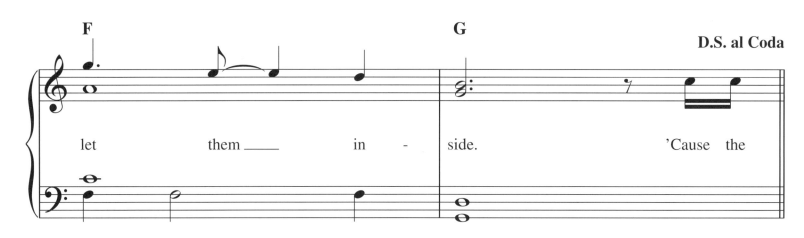

D.S. al Coda

let them _____ in - side.   'Cause the

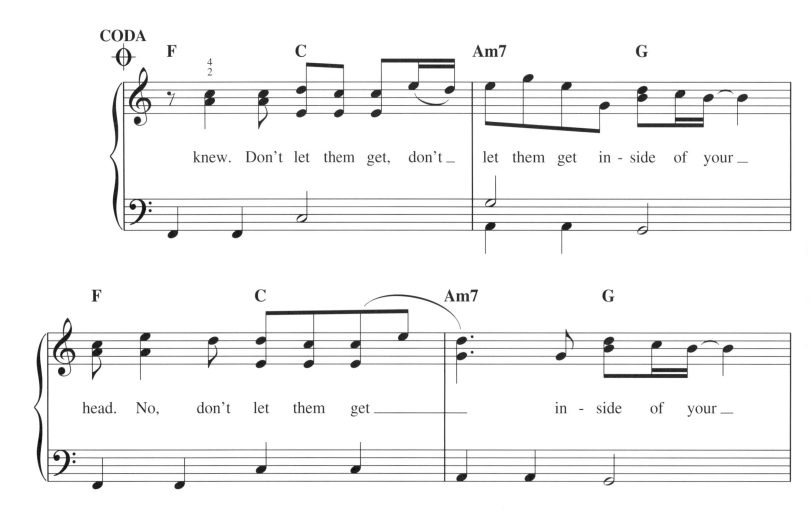

CODA

knew. Don't let them get,   don't _ let them get in - side of your _

head.   No,   don't let them get _____ in - side of your _

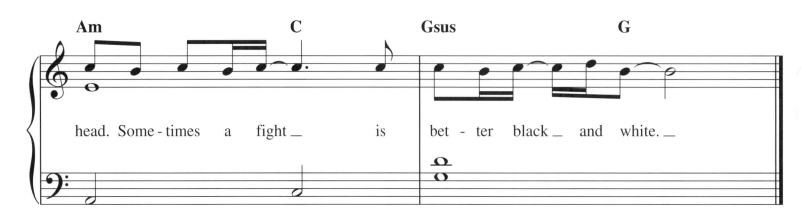

head. Some - times   a   fight _ is   bet - ter black _ and   white. _

DON'T CHARGE ME FOR THE CRIME

Words and Music by NICHOLAS JONAS,
JOSEPH JONAS, KEVIN JONAS II,
LONNIE RASHID LYNN JR. and RYAN LIESTMAN

Moderate Rock, with a groove

Rap: The

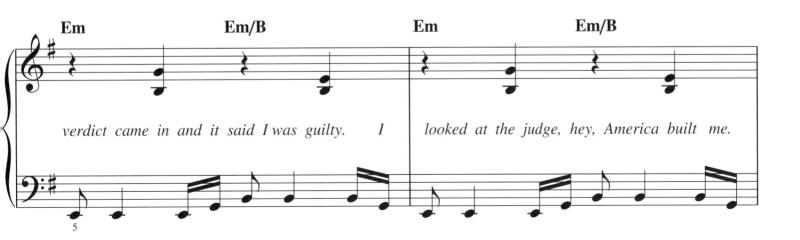

verdict came in and it said I was guilty.   I

looked at the judge, hey, America built me.

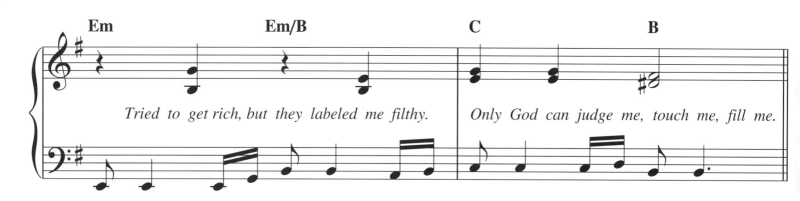

Tried to get rich, but they labeled me filthy.

Only God can judge me, touch me, fill me.

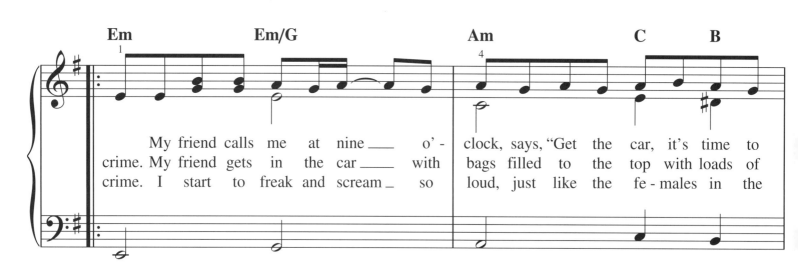

My friend calls me at nine ___ o'-clock, says, "Get the car, it's time to
crime. My friend gets in the car ___ with bags filled to the top with loads of
crime. I start to freak and scream _ so loud, just like the fe - males in the

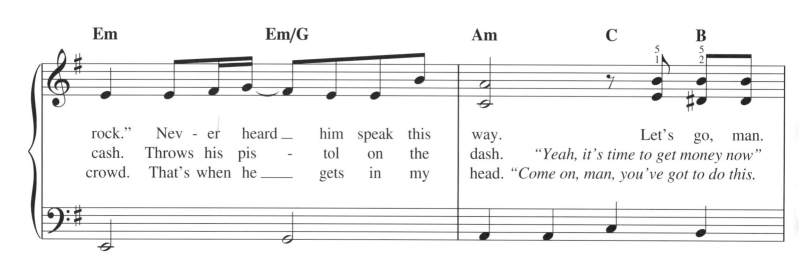

rock." Nev - er heard _ him speak this way.   Let's go, man.
cash. Throws his pis - tol on the dash.   *"Yeah, it's time to get money now"*
crowd. That's when he ___ gets in my head. *"Come on, man, you've got to do this.*

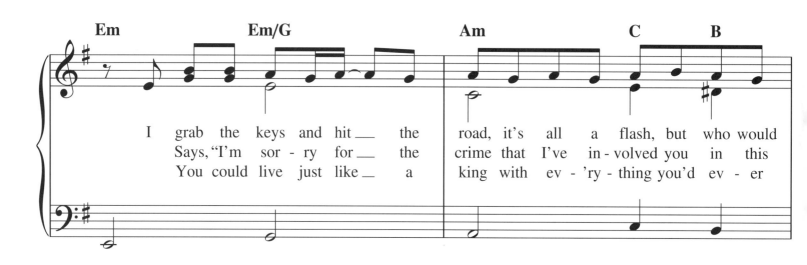

I grab the keys and hit ___ the road, it's all a flash, but who would
Says, "I'm sor - ry for ___ the crime that I've in - volved you in this
You could live just like _ a king with ev - 'ry - thing you'd ev - er

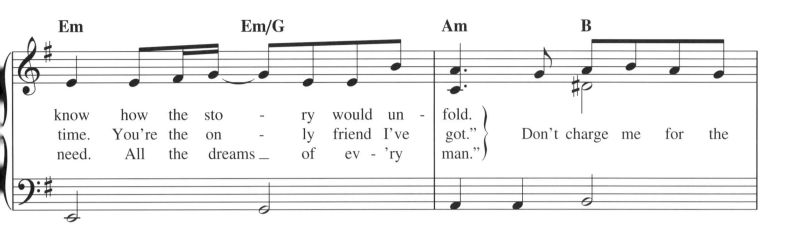

know how the sto - - ry would un - fold.
time. You're the on - - ly friend I've got." } Don't charge me for the
need. All the dreams __ of ev - 'ry man." }

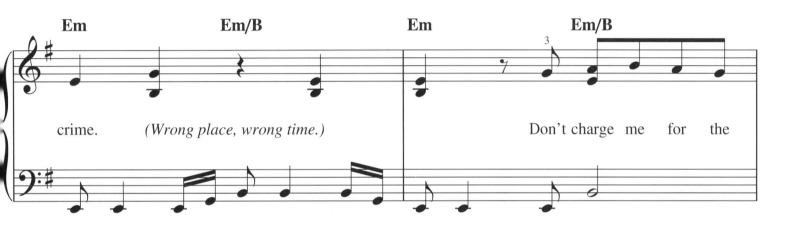

crime.   *(Wrong place, wrong time.)*

Don't charge me   for   the

1., 2.

crime. _____   *(Wrong place, wrong time.)*

Don't charge me   for   the

3.

Don't charge me...

Rap: Sirens sound and my heart was pounding, I

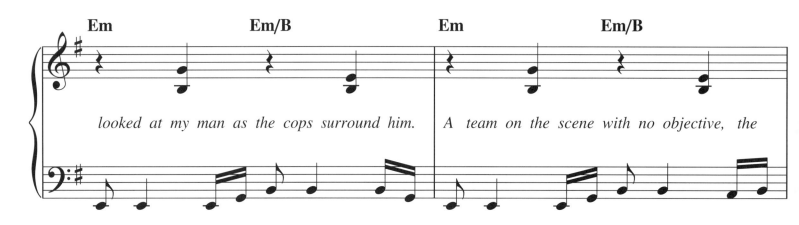

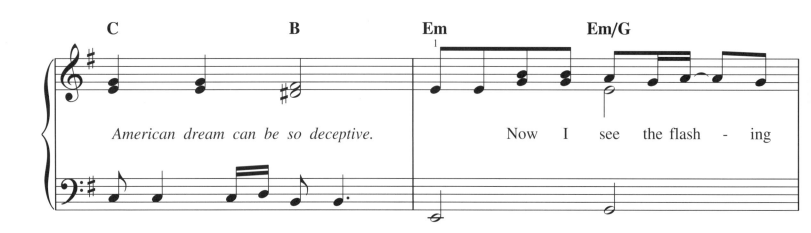

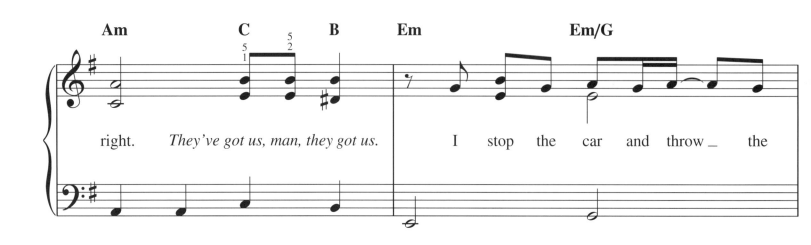

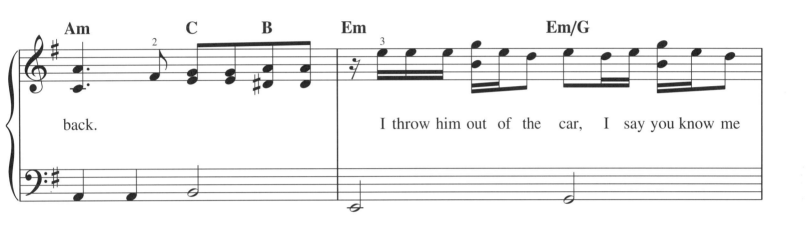

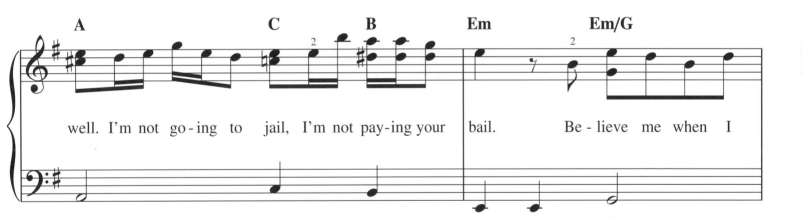

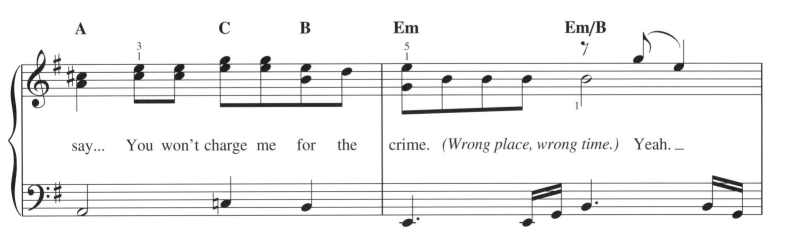

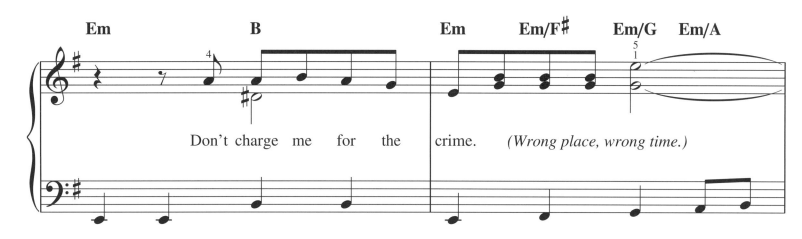

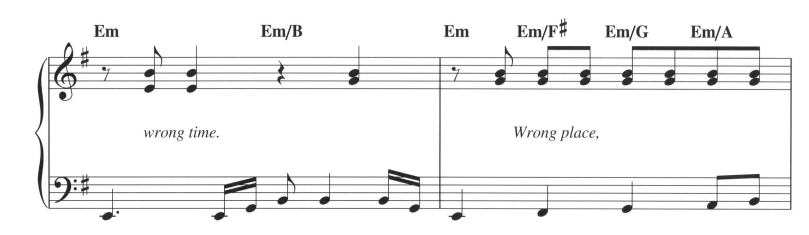

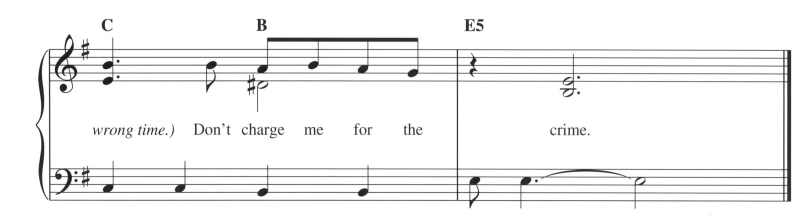

TURN RIGHT

Words and Music by NICHOLAS JONAS,
JOSEPH JONAS and KEVIN JONAS II

Pick up all your tears, ___
driv-ing all your friends ___ out at the

throw them in your back - seat.
speed you can-not fol - low, and

Leave with-out a sec - ond
soon you will be on ___ your

glance,
own. And

some - how I'm to blame ___ for this
some - how I'm to blame ___ for this

nev - er - end - ing race - track you call life. _____
nev - er - end - ing race - track you call life. _____

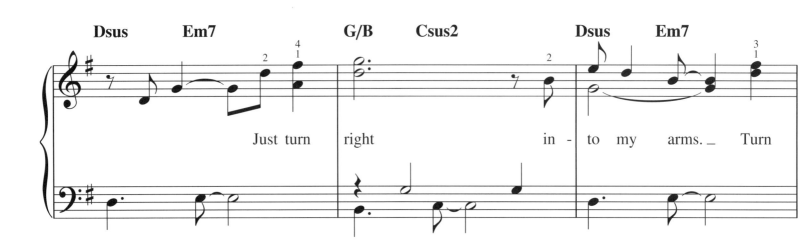

Just turn right in - to my arms. _ Turn

right, _____ you won't be a - lone. _ You might

fall off this track _ some - times, hope to see __ you on the fin - ish line.

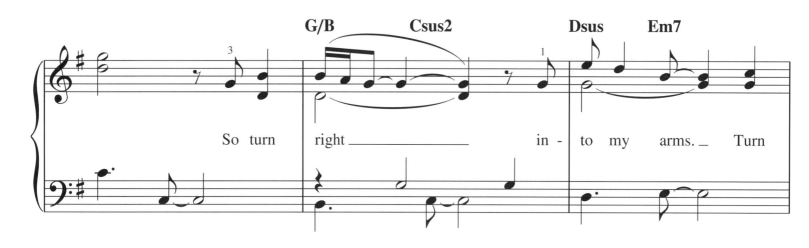

So turn right _____ in - to my arms. _ Turn

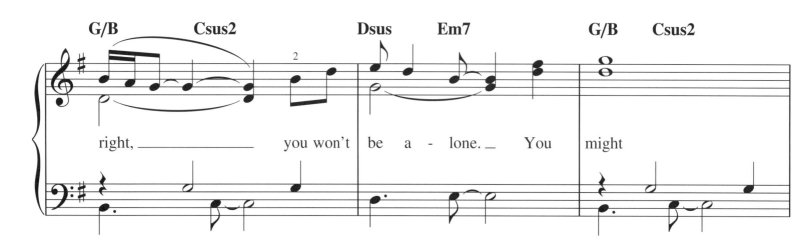

right, _____ you won't be a - lone. _ You might

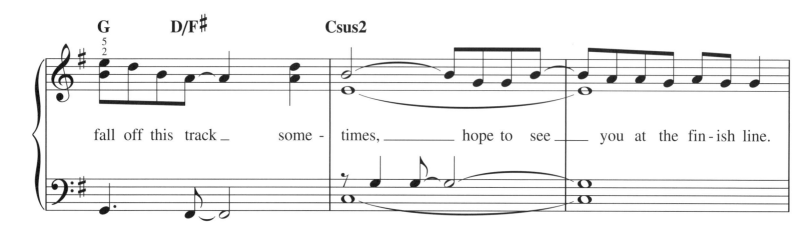

fall off this track _ some - times, _____ hope to see _ you at the fin - ish line.

DON'T SPEAK

Words and Music by NICHOLAS JONAS,
JOSEPH JONAS and KEVIN JONAS II

KEEP IT REAL

Words and Music by NICHOLAS JONAS,
JOSEPH JONAS and KEVIN JONAS II

There came a day ___
Who can know ___

when the songs ___ that you play ___ are
that you'll be ___ on the road, ___

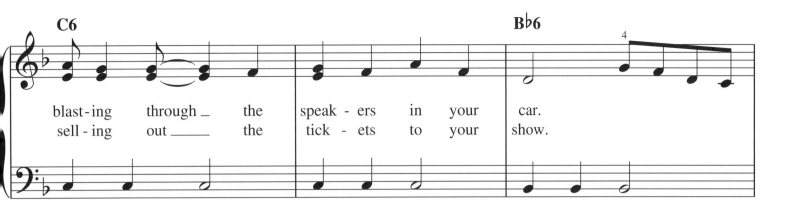

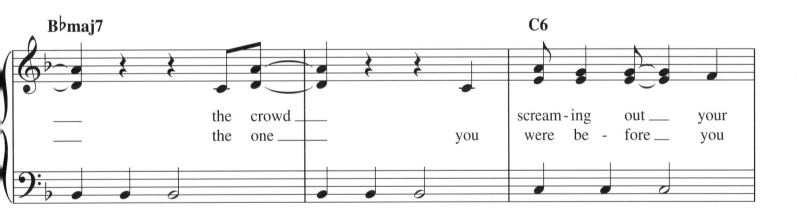

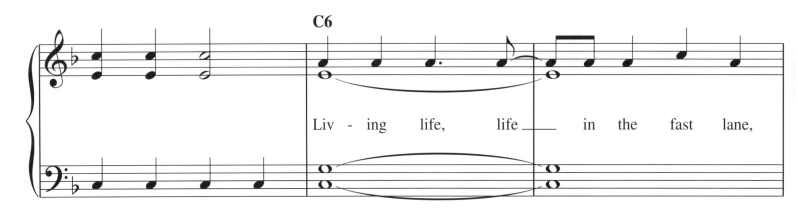

Liv - ing life, life in the fast lane,

not that bad, you know we can't com - plain. Who's to say that

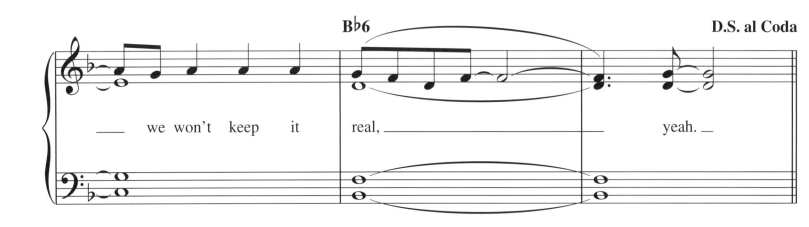

we won't keep it real, yeah.

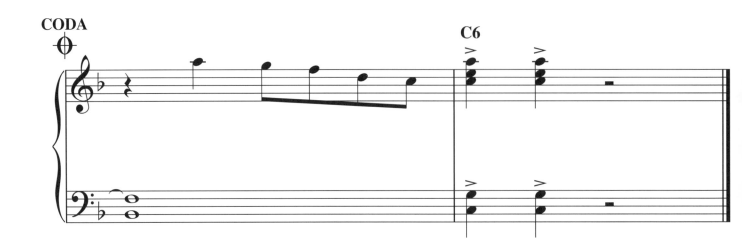